IMAGES OF ENGLAND

MACCLESFIELD

IMAGES OF ENGLAND

MACCLESFIELD

DOUG PICKFORD

TEMPUS

Frontispiece: Look to the right of this picture and the familiar face of John, now Sir John, Mills can be seen. He was filming *So Well Remembered* in Macclesfield for Hollywood's RKO Studios in 1946 and many Macclesfield folk had the thrill of appearing as extras; some being paid and many just there for the fun of being 'stars'. There are many familiar Macclesfield faces in this photograph, which was taken from a glass negative, watching the shooting of a scene at the side of the Union Gateway close to the Town Hall. The building in the background is The Feathers public house, a hostelry that many will recall but few will admit to having visited! In the background, just behind the Fosters van, can be seen a little of Seymour Meads shop in the Market Place. The film played to packed houses at the Majestic Cinema on its release and in the 1980s was shown again at the cinema, this time for a charity gala night, and proved just as popular.

First published 1998
Re-issued 2003

Tempus Publishing Limited
The Mill, Brimscombe Port,
Stroud, Gloucestershire, GL5 2QG

British Library Cataloguing in Publication Data.
A catalogue record for this book is available from the British Library.

ISBN 0 7524 3018 1

Typesetting and origination by Tempus Publishing Limited
Printed in Great Britain by Midway Colour Print, Wiltshire

Contents

Acknowledgements

Included in the public acknowledgement of my indebtedness for assistance in compiling this book are the people mentioned here. However, there are countless other Maxonians, far and near, who have shown much kindness to me by loaning their treasured old photographs. If I have not mentioned their names it is for no other reason than that my mind is too full. My sincere thanks to everyone: Geoffrey Hunter, Claire Crosby, Hilary Pickford, Paul Dunkley, Ursula Arden, Philip Foster (Byron Street), Mrs B. Eaton (Barton Street), Philip Smith, Chris Dorey, Mike Dorey, Mrs Hilda Bailey, Cyril Dawson, Derek Lockett, Margaret Lockett, Maurice Winnell, Jeff Collins, Mrs H. Mellor, Vera Read, Mrs M. Mason, Mr and Mrs Arthur Mellor (Park Lane), Mrs Muriel Massey (Holmes Chapel), John Bowyer, Mrs M. White, Mrs D. Hancock (Middlewich), Mr Keith Goalen, Mr Kenneth Armitt.

Introduction

I owe a great and sincere debt of gratitude to Tempus Publishing for approaching me to compile this book. It had not been my intention to produce any more Macclesfield-based books, as much as I dearly love the old town where I have spent many, many happy years. Rather, my sights were set on other horizons. However, our initial talk prompted me into action and no sooner had I sat down to contemplate 'Should I or shouldn't I?' than I answered the question. Of course I should. Macclesfield is where my heart is and I could not possibly say no.

For those who are not aware, and Macclesfield is such a changing township that there are probably very many, I began my writing associations at the turn of the decade of the 1960s when I began work at the old *Macclesfield Advertiser* under the late Harry Hayes. Not only did he teach me to respect and revere Macclesfield but he also taught me a great deal about its wealth and abundance of history. From there I was privileged to move 'across the road' to the wider circulation *County Express* which became the *Macclesfield Express*. There was at the time a great man in charge. His name was Clifford Rathbone and he wrote under the *nom de plume* of 'The Stroller'. Clifford's memory, like Harry's, possessed a huge reservoir of local knowledge and it was the combination of these two wonderful people which ignited the spark within me for 'Treacle Town'. This led me to not only produce four books of old Macclesfield but, on my retirement as editor of the *Express* after some 24 years at the helm, to help my dear wife Hilary with the publication of *Old Macc* magazine, another journal which taps the abundant spring of memories concerning this town. So, with four books about Macclesfield of old under my belt, the continuing story unfolding with the magazine and with countless articles I and other Maxonians had written for the newspapers over the years, it was perhaps no little wonder that I had decided not to produce any more. However, such is the pull on my heartstrings for the old town that here it is, and I am extremely pleased with the finished result.

Macclesfield is, as I have said, such an advancing and changing township that this kind of publication serves its inhabitants, both old and new, extremely well (I hope). I have endeavoured not to duplicate photographs within these pages that have already had an airing in public, and only the very odd one or two have slipped through for reasons of elaborating on events or suchlike. In the main they have never been published in book form. In fact, the ease in which some 200 plus 'new' old photographs came to me shows just what a treasure chest of Macclesfield memorabilia there is. I have said before that the town has struggled to retain its identity and I now feel that it is thanks to the pride within countless Maxonians that it has been able to win the battle, despite being ransacked, plundered and pillaged, changed here there and everywhere. But it's still 'Good Old Macc'.

The real stars shining within the pages of this book are the many Macclesfield people who have helped me over the years to piece together the Macclesfield of yesteryear through their recollections, their invaluable photographs and their sheer love of the town. They have provided treasures that cannot be matched. As editor of the local paper I was in the fortunate position of being able to speak to many people who possessed an abundant knowledge and photographic memories of the old place. I have made many lasting friendships in the process. My thanks go to them all, not least Geoffrey Hunter whose help, guidance and good nature have assisted me considerably. Geoffrey produced his own book *Waterloo Boy* a couple of years back and I was delighted to play a very small role in its eventual publication. This told of his boyhood and formative years in the Hurdsfield area of Macclesfield, an area now demolished, like so much of Macclesfield. It proved an immediate best seller and I am delighted for him.

Geoffrey has also assisted in no small way with this publication. I so well remember visiting his home one morning armed with a pile of photographs. These pictures were causing problems. I could either not identify the people on them, or the reason for their being taken in the first place eluded me. Or both. Geoffrey sat at his table with the pictures spread out in front of him. He picked up the first one. 'Ah, that's so and so' he said. 'And it's 1947, taken at such and such . . .'

He went through the lot in a short space of time, and wrote clear and concise captions to most of them.

One or two alluded both him and me but he was not going to be beaten. 'Leave them with me for a few days' he said, and I did. He must have spoken to many people throughout the town, showing them the photos and, I am pleased to report, it was 'mission accomplished'. He telephoned a few days later to report that he had been successful in not only identifying them but had even spoken to a lady who was pictured on one of them. Thanks Geoff.

There are many others whose paths have crossed with mine because of the publication of this volume. For instance, there is Paul Dunkley, another ex-Hurdsfield resident, who went on to the King's School through his own endeavours. His father, Eric, was an extremely well-known and respected local journalist in Macclesfield, before moving away to Leek, and the regard and esteem in which Eric was held has impressed me considerably. Through the good offices of his son, Paul, I am now able to bring to the public's attention some of the finest old photographs ever produced. One in particular should be mentioned, it is the first in this book, given pride of place because it is such a gem. It shows John Mills, now Sir John Mills, and the Hollywood film crew at a filming session near to that old and infamous pub The Feathers at the side of the Town Hall in 1946. Not only is it as clear as crystal but it shows many of the Macclesfield people who were extras in the film So Well Remembered. It is delightful. My great thanks go to him also. There are countless others who should be mentioned but to mention some and omit perhaps one or two would be unwise, so I shall thank them all personally.

I hope this book is able to show the many new folk within the town what a delightful place it was and still is and I also hope that the memories of thousands of Maxonians will perhaps be jolted a little by some of the pictures within. Please read and enjoy it as much as I have enjoyed bringing it to you.

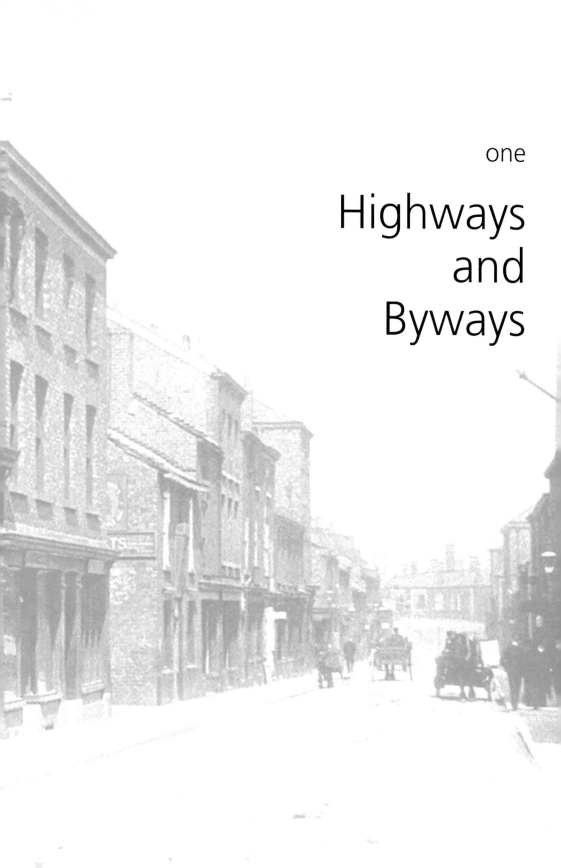

one

Highways
and
Byways

Above: A trip down Memory Lane to how things used to be. Here we take a look at Chestergate in the early part of the twentieth century. The building in the centre of the picture, with the lamp hanging from the wall was the Flying Horse Hotel, now an insurance office. Churchill Way now runs across the picture, left to right, between the Old King's Head and the Flying Horse. What was on the cart in the foreground? The baskets may possibly have contained laundry but it is also thought that they could have held vegetables. Just by the parked cart, on the right, there was a printer's shop down the alley way which was there certainly up until the 1960s.

One of the most architecturally delightful thoroughfares in Macclesfield is Park Lane. This junction with Oxford Road and Congleton Road is now dominated by traffic lights but back in the 1930s it was a quiet rural suburb.

Above: Further down towards town is a row of houses (right) erected in 1911 by James Eaton, and known as the Twelve Apostles. This photograph was taken shortly after the row was built.

Opposite below: A sad and sorry sight. Stanley Street, sometimes referred to as Dog Lane, pictured just before it was to be demolished to make way for the Grosvenor Shopping Precinct in 1969. The view shows Derby Street at the top, which became Churchill Way around the same time. In the foreground (left), is the building that housed one of Macclesfield's local papers, the County Express, and the printing side of the business, Macclesfield Press. This building was situated where Boots the Chemists now is in the shopping precinct. The buildings centre-left are now part of the multi-storey car park and formerly housed Arthur Bradbury & Son. Between these two buildings was the Macclesfield Conservative Club and, of course, the Stanley Hall where many a dance was held, many a romance blossomed and many a memory was made.

Left: The postcard says Beech Lane but this is in fact Manchester Road, Tytherington, in the 1940s. The road, the main route from Manchester to Derby and the South, became busier and busier as traffic increased until the Silk Road took away most of the through traffic in the early 1990s. Now it is partly returning to a tree-lined lane as depicted here.

Below: Another leafy lane on the outskirts of town is the road to Prestbury passing the West Park (right) and the old West Park hospital (left). The gas lamps and the lone cyclist stand witness to the date of the photograph which is around 1910.

Derby Street, now Churchill Way. Ashton's leather goods shop and Wm Smith & Son, pet food supplies, are pictured. The site is opposite what is now the Cheshire Building Society's fine Kerridge stone-built head offices which were, of course, formerly the Macclesfield General Post Office. The photograph was taken in the 1960s when much of Macclesfield was blighted because of promised new roads here, there and everywhere. To alleviate part of Macclesfield's traffic problem, Churchill Way was built from Park Street, along the route of Derby Street and towards the King's School gates. It was built shortly after the great statesman's death and was dubbed 'a road that started nowhere and finished nowhere'. Much property was only released from planning blight when the Macclesfield Relief Road was finalized a good few years later. It is now known as the Silk Road, a fitting tribute to Macclesfield's staple industry for centuries.

Chestergate, now pedestrianized, was once one of the main through routes used originally for stagecoaches and other means of travel to, of course, Chester and beyond. Many hostelries sprung up around it including this long-departed inn, the Bull and Gate, situated approximately where the Leek United Building Society office now stands.

Mill Lane was and still is a much travelled thoroughfare. Very close to Park Green was this tobacconists shop which during the early 1930s was run by Macclesfield Town FC's captain, Billy Johnston, who is pictured outside the shop. Notice that the window is bedecked with the Cheshire Senior Cup and other football paraphernalia. The postcard is signed by the much-loved skipper.

Right: Commercial Road has now been cut up, knocked down and moved about, but it was not always so. Here, horse-drawn delivery vans line up outside Arighi Bianchi & Co., the famous Macclesfield stores, in Commercial Road. The fine cast-iron four-storey building, built in 1864, is flourishing now as ever. The building to the left, having been burnt down earlier this century, has been replaced by a car park.

Below: W.H. Smith's shop, not the large retail concern of today, but a grocery and provision dealer which stood at the corner of Derby Street and Thomas Street. Mr Smith is standing at the doorway here in around 1920.

Neckwear's offices, now demolished, at the bottom of Whalley Hayes car park. The company also had buildings in King Edward Street. Here can be seen greenhouses and myriad plant pots in the foreground, and the Austin cars date the picture to the late 1940s or early 1950s. There were a number of houses where the corporation car park now stands and at the western end, where this picture was taken, there is now new housing development. A bridge connected the two Neckwear buildings.

Opposite above: Workmen repair a road sign after an accident at the end of Chestergate at the junction with Prestbury Road and Chester Road in the late 1950s.

Opposite below: Remember the North Western Road Car Company? The familiar red and cream buses were the main feature of Sunderland Street's bus depot and of Macclesfield's highways. Here a Weston Estate bus stands alongside one for the Moss Rose at the rear of the bus depot in the early 1950s.

Above: Park Green, when it was part of the main north-south trunk road in the very early 1960s. The Congregational church as it then was later became the United Reformed church and in the background is the now-demolished Depot Mill, the site of Macclesfield's first silk warehouse and probably the site of the first silk mill in the town.

Left: A young girl having tended to her bantam hens in the courtyard at the rear of the Bate Hall, Chestergate, at around the time of the First World War.

Gleave Motors, at the corner of Davenport Street and Buxton Road, now the site of Kwik Fit. The site was formerly occupied by the Royal Oak public house.

Commercial Road from the corner of North Street looking towards Norton Street and Gladstone Square. From the right: the door to the men's reading room upstairs, J. Rowbotham – men's hairdresser, Mrs Dean's sweet shop, Natty Whalley's toy shop, Miss Bellamy's ladies outfitters and post office, Holland's hardware shop. Further to the left was Palin's grocers and bakers and on the corner of Norton Street was The Woodman.

Some photographs of Broken Cross through the ages. The Co-op stands to the left, and the famous clock can be clearly seen at the rear. Dating back to around 1925, this postcard has had three telegraph poles removed by an artist, presumably to make the picture more appealing.

This turn of the century postcard is addressed to Miss Agnes Kellett, the Sanatorium, Southport and was sent by an S. Fisher. The picture shows a laden pony and trap trundling to the town centre.

A much older picture looking in the direction of Macclesfield. The posters on the wall advertise a sale of farming stock at Pool End Farm, Tytherington, and a gas lamp stands in the middle of the road. What a change from today.

Four children pose for the cameraman at Broken Cross in around 1910. This postcard was sent by James Bowyer of 36 Barton Street, Macclesfield, to his relatives at Upperhulme, near Leek. Mr Bowyer later became the Broken Cross policeman.

F.E. Russell's butchers in Park Green, now Marshall Spearings. The pork butchers was famous for its fine sausage and potted meats among other delicacies. The sign in the window says the day's special offers were pressed beef and pork pies. The pies had a richness and a savoury taste that was unique to this establishment and the pressed beef was praised for many a mile around. There were far more butchers' shops in the town in those days, most having now fallen victim to the supermarkets. When this photograph was taken in the late 1940s these superstores were unheard of and many people had their weekly orders delivered to their homes, usually by a young lad on a bicycle. Some would say we have progressed but others would disagree. I leave you to form your own opinion.

When traffic journeyed through the centre of Macclesfield early in the twentieth century, it was not traffic jams that had to be faced. Rather, it was the Market Place congested by stalls every day of the week save Sunday. This extremely rare photograph shows the many 'side stalls' that used to be around the perimeter of the bustling stalls. These were used mainly by farmers and country folk who brought their wares which included eggs, butter, cheese and vegetables. Although not in very good condition because of its age, the picture shows in graphic detail how those days now long gone used to be. These small stalls were displayed not just in front of the Town Hall and to the side, but around the Parish church, along the opposite side of the road by the Angel and northwards to the Bulls Head. There were sellers outside the old District Bank, now the library, and down Brunswick Street as well.

There were, as Maxonians are only too aware, two railway stations in Macclesfield at one time. The station known as Hibel Road is pictured here, so-named because its approach began on that road. There was also what is the present Central Station. The LMS railway was at the corner of, appropriately enough, Station Street. This was by far the busiest of the town at one point, carrying most of the goods from here. The next few pictures show those wonderful halcyon days of steam through pictures by Martin Welch, courtesy of John Williams. How many recall the sweets and tobacconists shop on Hibel Road, from where this picture was taken, and what about the Railway Inn just up the road? It has all now gone under the demolition man's hammer. A Tesco superstore now stands on the site of Hibel Road goods yard and station.

Opposite above: A Manchester-London express, Britain Class, Charles Dickens, going past Potts' coal yard.

Opposite below: Macclesfield Central Station in the early 1950s. What a pity the steam engines had to make way for diesel and, later, electric engines. Cleaner they may be but the sight, sound and smell of steam and smoke was a sensual pleasure.

Hibel Road, showing the turntable which was used for trains that came through from Staffordshire on the old Knotty Line, the North Staffordshire Railway, and turned around at Hibel Road to journey south again.

The year is 1936 and local railwaymen tend a London Midland Scottish 2-6-2.

A steam train chugs into the newly-refurbished Central Station after the Hibel Road passenger station had closed. This engine may possibly have been bound from or to the Bollington, Higher Poynton line.

Hibel Road top yard, 1949. From left to right: Martin Lafferty, Bill Cotton (Shunter), Donald Campbell, -?-, Len Houghton, Frank Shelley.

From the glorious age of steam we journey to the tranquil days of the canal. Macclesfield Canal is as busy now as ever, with leisure craft and very little, if any, commercial traffic navigating the waterway. But it was not always so. Up until the Second World War and beyond, Macclesfield Canal, like so many others, was a hive of activity with barges going to and fro carrying all sorts of goods from coal to iron, fertilizer to textiles. Here we see Mr John Green of Macclesfield (nearest to the barge) who died in the 1980s. His house can be seen in the background of the shot. Mr Green's haulage company comprised horses and barges. During the 1930s, when this picture was taken, his barges carried coal, as well as paper for Backhouse & Coppock of Sutton.

Opposite above: Green's Road and canal haulier's wharf on the Macclesfield Canal, adjacent to the Hovis Mill.

Opposite below: Another view of the Macclesfield Canal and the Hovis Mill, with the placards on the wall telling canal traffic that Hovis was invented in 1886. This Bullock Brothers postcard was taken in around 1910.

Sunderland Street and Park Green used to house the offices of the London and North West Railway's district traffic superintendent. It was also a stopping-off point for old British buses, whose depot was in King Edward Street, as well as being the centre for Macclesfield Equitable Provident Society. This 'boneshaker' of a bus was on its way to Congleton shortly after the First World War. Just look at those tyres – hardly conducive to a smooth ride, especially along this highway which used to be between the two townships. Many of the curves and bumps have been taken away today, but these passengers were certainly in for a bumpy ride.

Opposite above: Green's hauliers' barge outside their house on the Macclesfield Canal near to Black Road.

Opposite below: All was not always so tranquil. The year is 1931 and one of Green's motor vehicles, used to transport goods from the canal to the final destination, is on fire. Mr John Green is pictured, right, watching the hosepipe being trained on the smouldering remains.

Chestergate with flags waving and bunting flying, viewed from the Market Place. The occasion was, it is thought, Empire Day.

This postcard was sent during the First World War and invites the recipient to a variety theatre in the Potteries. It shows Mill Street from the Park Green direction. The post box, centre of picture, is still in the same position and the sign above proclaims the British and Foreign Bible Society depot.

The Peels Arms sign hangs to the left of this photograph as children gather around a pony and cart delivering milk. The date is around the First World War. Milk used to be delivered in churns and ladled out with beautiful copper scoops into household wares such as jugs or bowls. Recollections may be playing tricks but the liquid seemed to be much creamier when delivered that way. Mind you, it was before the milk was pasteurised, homogenised or sterilised.

Crompton Road has changed very little since this photograph was taken in around 1920. The cobbles have made way for tarmac and the gas lamps have now become electric. The railings on the stone walls have gone now – victims of the war effort in the 1940s. Oh, and the road, like every other, has now been taken over by the motor car.

Sunderland Street, Macclesfield, taken around the year 1908. The Co-operative Furnishing Department is to the left. The delivery boy to the front of the premises has parked his bicycle behind him and is carrying a parcel, the contents of which are a mystery. The lady to the right is standing under the Brook Street sign. At the rear of this fine photograph, the old Central Station buildings can just be seen. Two horse-drawn carts pass each other and a handcart is pushed past the George and Dragon. All the buildings to the right housed Macclesfield Equitable Provident Society stores ranging from furnishings to provisions. The department in view would have displayed cured hams, smoked bacons, large cheeses and chests of exotic teas from the colonies. What a glorious collection of smells must have emitted from that building! Perhaps the delivery boy was on his way from there, but more likely he was taking cloth to a household in Macclesfield.

Opposite above: There can be very few photographs taken of Ryles Park Road before it became a road proudly containing fine houses. Here we can see that the first houses had been built and trees had just been planted on the side of the pavement. The field on the right was later built upon and now houses Ryles Park High School. The view was taken shortly before the Second World War.

Opposite below: A view from Queen Victoria Street over to the Parish church and Town Hall. Backwallgate goes off at the bottom of the picture to the right towards Mill Street. The building on the left is now Brian Ollier's photographic studios. The cars date the picture to the early 1960s and there is an old school sign on the road, centre bottom, presumably for Mill Street School (the entrance being from Boden Street at the bottom of Queen Victoria Street).

The bottom of Hurdsfield looking up towards the Durham Ox. The shop on the right on the corner of Blagg Street, now demolished, used to be Nield's newsagents – also sellers of sweets and tobacco. On the retirement of Mr and Mrs Bill Nield in the 1930s, son Jack and his wife Lily took over the shop. Further up on the right was the Hanging Gate public house. Gas Road is off to the left. The boys in the centre have no fear of traffic. They happily pose for the photographer and are dressed in high collars and suits, not the everyday wear of young lads in those days. So perhaps they had been to Sunday school, or knew the photograph was to be taken and their mums had made sure they would be presentable. Two of them are carrying striped canes. What game were they playing? A window cleaner's ladders are parked outside the Hanging Gate. Perhaps he was cleaning the windows inside, or perhaps he was cleaning the glasses out inside!

Opposite above: More pictures of the Hurdsfield area. Here we see Arbourhey Street, now demolished. The shop the boys are standing outside of is facing Fence Avenue, opposite, and on the corner was the Elephant and Castle pub.

Opposite below: Leigh Street, Hurdsfield, in October of 1958. At this time the area was blighted and the Clearance Order had been made, eventually to uproot families that had been in the area for centuries.

Norton Street in 1958, taken from Arbourhey Street. The net curtains are tastefully draped and it is obvious that the occupants were extremely house-proud. Again, this street is with us no longer.

Queen Street leading into Commercial Road showing the Steam Bakery, as it was in the 1930s and 1940s, which was kept by the Leah family who resided in Steeple Street. On the opposite corner was the old Bird in Hand pub which later became a private house.

Commercial Road taken from near to where the cattle pens were built, close to the bridge under Gas Road. The Bedford van was owned by Abel Heywood, wholesale newsagents.

A panoramic view of Hurdsfield Road before the many houses were built. What a different view this would be today with the industrial estate, new roads and houses. The Kerridge hills are in the background.

Over to the other side of town and a return to Park Lane. The houses on the right have now come down and the horse manure in the middle of the road shows what form of transport there used to be. The buildings, centre, are still there and the house with the steps to the left is intact. Those lovely trees have been pruned away and the college grounds now stand at the rear of those trees. The park the road was named after was South Park, although close to where Ryles Park school now is (named after the man who gave the park land to the town) there was, centuries before, a stronghold in a hunting park used by the Saxon and Norman lords. Little has ever been found of this and perhaps much still lies under the soil waiting to be discovered.

Opposite above: Chester Road, looking towards Broken Cross. The lad leaning on the lamp-post perhaps waiting for a 'certain little lady to pass by' is situated outside the shop that later became Harry Williamson's off-licence. There is now a roundabout outside the Card Factory at the back of this picture.

Opposite below: A view of Gas Road from Brunswick Hill, with a fine steam engine passing Arighi Bianchi's building in Commercial Road in the background. Some of the posters along the road can be identified. For instance, there is Kit-e-Kat, Omo, Capstan cigarettes, a railway poster, Mackeson, and one that tells us we can 'Rely on Relay', meaning Radio Relay the Macclesfield company that piped radio and later television to thousands of homes.

What a wonderful panoramic view of The Waters, Macclesfield. This horse fair was photographed around the 1920s and shows the buying and selling of not only horses but cattle as well. It may well have been a hiring fair also, where farm hands would stand and be hired for a year by farmers. Just look at some of the characters talking in groups, looking over the livestock or just standing and staring. The parish church of St Michael's and All Angels stands commandingly above, and pubs such as the Nag's Head, Chain and Gate, Old Millstone and Bull and Gate await the chance to quench the thirsts of those

visiting the market. The hoardings under Jacob's Ladder, centre left, announce the Hippodrome, Oxford Street. It is just possible to see crowds of people in the background; these would have been looking at either market stalls or perhaps some of the 'come-ons' or freak shows that used to tour and visit the markets at special times of the year. This photograph is thought to have been taken during the Macclesfield Wakes Selling Fair in early October, just before the trees on the slope under the church lost their leaves.

The main road in and out of Macclesfield for countless centuries went through the Market Place and by the Town Hall, previously the Guild Hall. This 1890s photograph shows the Unicorn Gateway (left) which led to many shops, pubs and houses at the rear of the Town Hall, including the Unicorn public house. The Bull's Head, a former staging hostelry for the Stage and Post coaches, is on the right, and the front of the Town Hall can be seen in the background as can some of the market stalls. The fact that the stalls are all together and not being used suggests the picture was taken on a Sunday, the only day of the week that stalls were not in full swing in the Market Place, except Good Friday and Christmas Day. This area used to contain a market cross which was later used as a roller on a farmer's field. The cross was taken into West Park for a number of years and is now situated outside the Parish church. Although not now in its original position, it is close to where it used to be (in front of the Town Hall). It was here that Bonnie Prince Charlie made the Mayor proclaim The Young Pretender monarch of England and it was from here that countless other proclamations have been made throughout the centuries.

two

School
and
Scouts

The morning milk break for the juniors of Ash Grove School. This early to mid 1950s picture should provide happy memories for many. The milk break required milk monitors and looking at this picture the children also had biscuits as well while seated at their desks. The half pint bottles were poured into plastic cups and this practice continued until the 1980s.

With ribbons and bows and their best pinafore dresses, these girls of St George's School, Macclesfield, pose for the class picture in 1906. The headmaster, left, was Mr Salt and the teacher, right, was Miss Potts.

Boys of Christ Church School, Macclesfield, during the King's jubilee year, 1935. Headmaster Mr Simpson is pictured with, back row, left to right: Dennis Wallace, Kenneth Pointon, Bob Walton, Stanley Oakes, Alan Nixon, Ronald Thornley. Middle row: Brian Cooke, Les Bracegirdle, Philip Dixon, Colin Sparkes, Wilfred Sherrat, Raymond Goodall. Front row: John Baxter, Philip Hannaghan, Gerald Barnes, Stanley Crankshaw, Derek Palmer.

Curls and ringlets were certainly in fashion for these young ladies of Christ Church School, Macclesfield, in 1910. The headmistress, right, was Mrs Beach.

Mill Street Higher Grade School in Lower Exchange Street, 1907. This boys' class certainly looked a smart lot with their large starched collars and a couple of them were even wearing buttonholes of flowers. Fifth from the right at the front is Ernest Farrar who, for the last 20 years of his life, kept the off-licence at Waterloo Street until it was demolished. Also in the picture is Edmund Lomas of the silk mill family and it is understood that a member of the Scragg family of Ernest Scragg & Sons is also pictured.

Macclesfield Central School boys' visit to BSA works on 14 June 1933. BSA were better known later for their motor bikes, but here the Macclesfield pupils are gathered around a brand new BSA tourer.

Daybrook Street Boys' School, Macclesfield, with teacher Mr Norman Tattersall in the 1950s. The boys on the front row are seated on PE mats made from rushes, which many will recall perhaps not with affection, but certainly with nostalgia.

Mill Street School was a happy place for many Maxonians and many people will recall with affection the headmistress, Miss Pocknall, who is thought to be the lady on the right of the picture, inside the school with a government inspector and two of the pupils during the 1940s.

A mixed class of boys and girls of various ages at Bridge Street Wesleyan School in the early part of the twentieth century. The headmaster at the time was Mr John Earles who is remembered today for his famous book Streets and Houses of Old Macclesfield.

St George's schoolrooms, Macclesfield, closed in the late 1980s after over a century of use and after countless numbers of children had been educated in its hallowed halls. This photograph was taken some time during the later years of Queen Victoria's reign and shows the staff inside the main classroom. The desks with holes in which the ink wells were placed are neatly lined up and one teacher is leaning on a fine piano which would have accompanied many a school assembly, religious service and Friday afternoon singing lessons. Gas mantles adorn the walls and, from where the photographer has taken his picture, there was a large coke-burning black metal stove. Perhaps some former pupils may recall the teachers standing with their backs to this fire during the winter months as they lectured the pupils.

Everyone had a great time at this hilarious Gang Show back in the 1950s with some of the older lads going Hawaiian style to add to the treat for the audience.

Fun and games Gang Show style with Raymond Maddock in the centre certainly having a load of laughs.

A 9th Macclesfield St John's Gang Show in the 1950s. Among the scouts and cubs shown here are: Brian Haley, John Sherratt, David Potts, Brian Rose, Norman Oldfield, Raymond Maddock, Peter Ellis, Elvin Birch, John Ellis, Ronald Barton, Derek Smith, Philip Norton, David Kwiakowski, Raymond Henry, David Smith, Graham Wilson, Christopher Davenport, Roger Tyrie, Paul Bamford, Roy Marshall. Also pictured, top-centre, is the leader Mr Kwiakowski.

High jinks at a Macclesfield Gang Show, 18 November 1952. Some of those pictured are: Ray Barton, Barry Swindells, Trevor Davis, John Gidman, Barry Truman, Brian Miller, Miss Hannon, -?- Lester, the Revd Robinson.

Off to camp – members of St Michael's Scouts and Cubs before they embarked on a happy trip during the early 1950s. Their transportation was supplied by Carswell's Parcel Express of Hurdsfield.

The Union Jack flies proudly in Victoria Park, Macclesfield, as families and friends watch the annual Macclesfield Scouts' and Guides' jamboree in the early 1950s.

Hurdsfield Cubs' Sermons Parade passing along Brocklehurst Avenue in 1959. There are many faces in this photograph that will be recognizable to Macclesfield people.

Another Hurdsfield parade during the 1950s, also a Sermons Parade, wending its way to Hurdsfield church.

three

Carnival Time

An early Macclesfield Carnival and one of the most historic and interesting photographs. The time is the 1930s when the carnival was in full swing, raising money for Macclesfield Infirmary. This was one of the floats, a lovely landau, lined up in Cumberland Street waiting for the procession to commence. These gentlemen were the 'genuine and original' Silk Lads, members of the very first Macclesfield Town Football Club team of the 1890/91 season. Second only to the Silk Queen herself, these elderly chaps took pride of place in the parade. The banner at the side proudly proclaims they had won the cup in 1890, 1891 and 1894. In those days the Silk Lads were known as the Lilly Whites because of the strip they wore which was all white. It was only after the Second World War that the Silkmen, as they became, wore the familiar blue and white strip we know today.

Pretty maids all in a row. There is no indication what mill these Little Bo Peeps represent, and just where their sheep are we can only surmise. They are gathered in Cumberland Street and pictured just before the parade commenced.

Above left: 'Snapshots in time'. A nurse approaches this photographer armed with a collecting box for the Infirmary funds in Park Lane. The year was 1933 and the young chap on the fine horse looked a splendid sight in the parade.

Above right: A beautifully bedecked bicycle in the parade down Park Lane. Just look at the two lads who have secured for themselves a grandstand view of the passing spectacle, top left. The lady spectator, right, awaits the rest of the procession and her young child, just in the picture, right, is waving a silk pompom.

Left: A snapshot of the Macclesfield Silk Queen, possibly Iris Barnes, as her float is driven along Park Lane, with a blacked-up collector walking by the spectators. The lad wearing a cap and possibly pushing a bike was a telegraph boy for the Post Office, showing that all walks of life took part in the grand parade.

Above: A.W. Hewetson's Beach and Lido Girls pictured in South Park after the parade. Judging by the certificates attached to the float, this was a prize-winning entry. Each and every silk mill in the town not only put forward a silk princess, one of whom was adjudged to be the Silk Queen, but also put forward floats or jazz bands or suchlike. The parade was very popular.

Left: A Silk Queen and her magnificent float, surrounded by Silk Princesses. It is obvious that an enormous amount of work had been put into not only the decoration of the float but in the lovely silk dresses worn by the ladies.

This motley crew were all members of Dunkerley's Mill Prize Jazz Band. In all sorts of fancy dress ranging from guardsman uniforms to Red Indians and clowns, they were certainly colourful characters. The drums, trombones, trumpets and other musical instruments ensured they added even more to the carnival atmosphere.

J. Wellings & Sons Builders entered this float during the 1933 parade and it is pictured here passing by the Infirmary. The sedan chair was, presumably, depicting the famous chair owned by a relation of Charles Roe which was kept in the Parish church for many years. Perhaps it was the original sedan chair, who knows!

Hovis, the famous bread born and bred in Macclesfield (well, almost, it in fact was invented in Stone, Staffordshire, but the entire production moved to Macclesfield where it was adopted by the town) entered this interesting float. Sacks of Hovis flour and figures of Hovis bakers were combined to brighten this fine vehicle.

Silk Queen Brenda Goodwin (probably) was driven in style to the parade and here we see her surrounded by admiring crowds as she arrives at the start of the parade. The photograph was taken by Mr F.R. Gee, newsagent, of 8 Roe Street, Macclesfield.

With banners such as 'Don't put on the Infirmary, putt on the green', and 'Help the Infirmary', these collectors roped in a Fyffes Bananas lorry to put over their point and presumably they raised a tidy sum for Macclesfield's hospital.

Weary Bill, searching for Halley's Comet, pushed his bike in the parade and was photographed in the park afterwards. This character, whose burnt-cork face would be frowned upon today, was the subject of much mirth and merriment at the time.

During the march of Bonnie Prince Charlie, the Young Pretender, southwards in 1745, Macclesfield was visited by thousands of Scottish troops. On the army's return a few days later, after they turned back at Derby, the town was visited by them again. Much has been written about that famous time when most of the townspeople lived in fear of their lives and when the Mayor was made to proclaim the Pretender rightful monarch of England. During one of the 1930s carnivals, this group, presumably from a local mill, bedecked themselves in tartan to relive the '45 Rebellion and the Macclesfield connection. They were photographed in the grounds of the Infirmary before the parade, and the gentleman in the centre is presumed to be Prince Charles Edward Stuart.

four

People

A typical and indeed a well-known Macclesfield family in around 1931. The Smith family lived at 18 Statham Street at the time and here we see Agnes and Arthur Smith with Josephine (Jo), Winifred, Gerald, Veronica, Philip, Monica, Margaret and the eldest child, Bertha. The girls all have typical hair styles of the era, as do the boys, and their highly polished shoes show how much pride people took in their appearances in those days.

Many Macclesfield people will recall Dorey's florists and greengrocers shop in Old Park Lane. Here we see Albert Edward Dorey and on the right, George Dorey, at a Drill Hall show in the early 1900s.

This is how Dorey's shop looked in 1906. In the picture are, left to right: an unnamed helper, Ada May Dorey, Grahame Dorey (who went on to run Gleave Motors), Albert Edward Dorey.

The date is September 1967 and the occasion is the farewell party for long-serving worker Mrs Potts at Glegg Street Day Nursery. Included on the photograph are Susan Corbishley, Mrs Hilda Bailey, Barbara Hogarth, Miss Robinson, Mary Baskerville, Miss Cockayne, Mrs Potts, Sister Capper, Susan Jones, Mrs Roberts (Matron), Nurse Lois.

Macclesfield Methodist Circuit Ministers in Victoria Park in 1898. Back row, left to right: the Revd E.Q. Buchanan, Revd E. Brentnall MA. Front row: Revd W. Brookes, Revd D. Young, Revd C.W. Prest (Superintendent).

Macclesfield High School girls, c. 1950, after their prize-giving ceremony.

Right: A choir procession in Mill Street, in the late 1940s or early 1950s. In the centre is Derek Hancox. The boys are standing outside MacDonald's hairdressers and Gregory's store.

Below: A fine body of men outside the Parish church in March of 1936. These were the Macclesfield Borough Police Force and the Chief Constable was Mr Shearsby. The Borough, or the township of Macclesfield, had its own police force in those days and the rural policing was carried out by the Cheshire Constabulary. PC Charles Lockett is on the second row from the front, third from the right. He was the father of well-known Maxonian Derek Lockett, who is to be thanked for this photograph.

Another fine body of men – the town's firemen lining up in King Edward Street prior to the Mayor's Sunday procession in November 1924.

Macclesfield mill workers, ladies all, line up before their annual outing from Clapham's shirt mill in Athey Street. A sign on the wall, far right, says 'Girls Wanted, experienced machinists aged over 18'. The date is probably late 1940s or early 1950s.

Some familiar faces on this trip organized by Mr Allison to Scotland from Rainow church on Bullock's coaches in the late 1940s.

The gentlemen are wearing bow ties and dinner jackets, the ladies their best ball gowns, for this Rotary Club of Macclesfield dance at the Stanley Hall. The Master of Ceremonies was Rotarian Jimmy Lomas.

Above: Another happy group at the same Rotary Club of Macclesfield annual charity dance at the Stanley Hall, Macclesfield.

Left: Three little girls caught in time. They are standing in Park Street around the year 1909 and perhaps one or more of them has paid a visit to Parker's dental surgery on the left, behind the railings. This stood where the former London and Manchester House grounds now are in Park Street, on the left as you look up towards Park Lane.

The old Macclesfield Board of Guardians pose for an official photograph at West Park hospital just before they were disbanded as the National Health Service took over their powers in 1948. These venerable ladies and gentlemen used to be responsible for, among other things, the Macclesfield Workhouse.

Employees of Macclesfield Slipper Mill at their annual Christmas party around 1959. The works used to be situated at the bottom of Hurdsfield and moved to Sunderland Street after a fire at Lower Heyes.

A Mill Street Town Mission (formerly City Mission) outing in the late 1920s. Back row, from left to right: Mr Gee, Mr Clowes, Cllr Butters, Missioner Mr Storey. Middle row, fourth along: Mrs Clowes, M. Stanway, Mrs Appleby, Mr Appleby. Front row includes: Mrs Gee, Mrs Butters, Mrs Storey, Mr Brown.

There are some very familiar Macclesfield faces here. Employees of Brocklehurst-Whiston Amalgamated with certificates of long service at a presentation ceremony in the 1960s.

A familiar face at many fêtes, rose queen ceremonies and carnivals during the 1920s, 1930s and 1940s was this gentleman, Tom Albinson of Macclesfield, who provided the music and commentary at many varied functions. Initially he used this enormous gramophone and loudspeaker and later moved on to slightly more sophisticated equipment.

The Macclesfield Adelphi Players were familiar faces in the town after the Second World War and into the early 1950s, being based at the Brocklehurst Memorial Hall, also known as the Liberal Club and, later, the El Rio Dance Hall. Here we see two members of the cast during rehearsals. The young lady is Jean Alexander who later became famous in Coronation Street and then for her cameo roles in Last of the Summer Wine and other series.

Above: A charabanc owned by Mr John Eccles of the Derby Arms, Chestergate, waits in the early 1930s in Park Green with these Macclesfield ladies and gentlemen aboard, before setting off for a destination thought to be Shrewsbury Flower Show.

Left: An unknown young lady depicting the fashions of the late 1950s pauses for a snapshot in Park Green. In doing so, much of Macclesfield's history is preserved for posterity because at the rear of the photograph is the old Silk Depot Mill, probably the first silk mill in Macclesfield, which is now long gone. A poster over what is now Spearing's butchers shop proclaims that it is 'Guinness Time'.

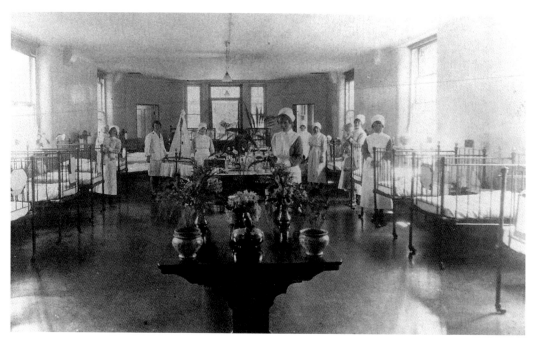

Two photographs of Macclesfield's glorious nurses in days now gone. This shows the children's ward at Macclesfield General Infirmary in 1925. Sister Dixon is to the fore and the nurse on the left, holding the baby, is Nurse Jones, the mother of well-known Maxonian Mrs Margaret Lockett.

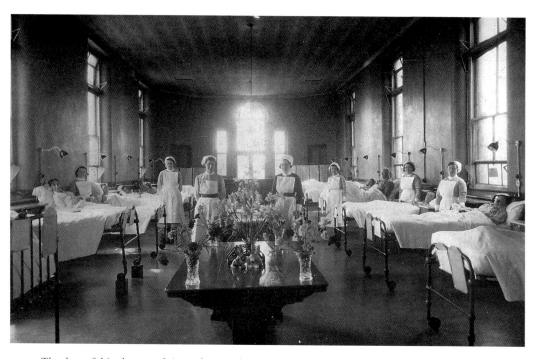

The date of this photograph is not known, but it is most certainly the men's ward at the Infirmary, probably in the late 1920s.

Opening Ceremony.

SECOND DAY :

Thursday, September 19th,

AT 3 P.M.

THE BAZAAR will be opened by

His Worship . . .
The Mayor of Macclesfield.

CHAIRMAN : W. SMALE, Esq., C.C.

The Bazaar Orchestra will be in attendance.

• • • • •

Admission 1s.

After 6 p.m. 6d.

HYMN.

ALL people that on earth do dwell,
    Sing to the Lord with cheerful voice;
Him serve with mirth, His praise forth tell,
Come ye before Him and rejoice.

Know ye, the Lord is God indeed;
Without our aid He did us make;
We are His flock, He doth us feed;
And for His sheep He doth us take.

O enter, then, His gates with praise,
Approach with joy His courts unto;
Praise, laud, and bless His name always,
For it is seemly so to do.

For why? the Lord our God is good,
His mercy is for ever sure;
His truth at all times firmly stood,
And shall from age to age endure.

SCRIPTURE. | PRAYER.

Above: Back in the early 1920s, one of the most talked-about events in the social calendar was the annual Grand Bazaar which took place at the Drill Hall. Each year was a different theme and one of the grandest was the Durban Bazaar where everything had a Middle Eastern theme. The number of people pictured here shows the popularity of the event which raised money for charity.

Left: Part of a programme for the Grand Bazaar.

five

Places

The time is the late 1920s and not only is this fine building brand new, but so is the road. This is Castle Street a few years after it was built, joining Chestergate with Derby Street, which is now Churchill Way. The road was built in the early 1920s to accommodate the expanding and booming town centre. At the top end there stood, grandly, the new Macclesfield General Post Office, a purpose-built building made from the finest Kerridge stone. When it was no longer adequate for the needs of the GPO in the early 1970s it was placed on the market. Macclesfield's much-respected building society, The Cheshire, which had begun its life in Parrs Bank chambers at the corner of Market Place and Chestergate and then moved to the Mill Street end of the then new Castle Street, took over and revitalised the building, making it a dynamic head office for this enterprising society. Castle Street took its name from the proximity of Macclesfield's castle, or castellated mansion, the remains of which were still visible when this road was constructed.

A Bullock Brothers original photograph of the former Roe Street chapel and, in the background, the Large Sunday School. The houses, top centre, have now gone and the new Churchill Way cuts across where they stood.

Further along Roe Street was, and still is, this fine building which has now become the Silk Heritage Centre. The Large Sunday School, or Roe Street Sunday School, was built in 1814 and this 1914 picture shows the centenary celebrations. The lovely railing went as part of the Second World War scrap metal effort.

William E. Pickston's butchers shop in 1910. The premises were at 77 Mill Street and the corner of Roe Street and were there for many years after this photograph was taken. Mr Pickston, the founder, is at the doorway.

The White Lion Hotel at the corner of Mill Street and Duke Street in the early 1920s when Mr Thomas Pickford was not only the proprietor, but brewed his own ale at the rear of the premises as well.

There are some unfortunate marks on the negative of this picture, but they do not detract from the interest this shot holds for countless Maxonians. The shops in Mill Street, shown in the late 1950s very early 1960s, are from left to right: Norvic shoes, Burton Tailoring, Hames bakers, and part of Hadfield's renowned chemists and drysalters at the corner of Stanley Street. Burtons still goes under the same name, although there is no longer a dance hall over it. Hames took over from Weston's bakers, owned by Macclesfield's MP Sir Garfield Weston, a Canadian. Hadfields has now moved to Churchill Way because of the Grosvenor Centre development.

On the opposite side of the road to Hadfield's chemists in Stanley Street there used to be a general stores and, next door, London Tailors. Later, Redmans took over this building and Chester Twemlow tobacconists took over the tailoring establishment.

Gas Road took its name from the Corporation Gas Works, which had pride of place at the corner of Hibel Road for many a year until electricity became the order of the day. Here we see a pre-1900 view of the works, with a finger post showing the way to Whalley Bridge, Leek and Sutton.

We have seen Broken Cross on previous pages, but the old toll bar cottage, a familiar landmark for many years, has now disappeared and was certainly a well-known building in the town for centuries.

There was demolition of some well-known buildings in Roe Street during the 1970s to make way for the new Sainsbury's store, which has now moved to the site of the old infirmary. This road was a bustling adjunct to Mill Street, and many small shops graced the street. For many years Mr F.R. Gee had a newsagent's shop at the premises below where the window gapes wide open. It was, in fact, a newsagent's shop until demolition, but Mr Gee was well known not only for his shop but for the fact that he was also a photographer, well-known for taking portraits. He was also known for his work with the local newspapers of the 1930s and 1940s, especially the Courier and the Times, not to mention the Advertiser. It was only later that the Times and the Courier became the County Express, and the Advertiser was amalgamated with a merger in the early 1980s.

Another scene of the demolition of Roe Street viewed from Duke Street. Duke Street itself has seen many changes over the years and much demolition and rebuilding has taken place.

The Flower Pot Hotel on the corner of Ivy Lane and Congleton road is a bustling and thriving black and white timbered establishment. However, the original Flower Pot was slightly further along Congleton Road and was nothing like the fine building we know today. Here is the original Flower Pot taken before the First World War.

The Westminster Bank (left) on the corner of Chestergate and the Market Place, was formerly Parr's Bank. This lovely stone facia building was demolished in the 1960s to make way for a concrete and glass construction that is now the Natwest Bank. Some would say it was for the better and others have a different opinion. Here we see a bustling Chestergate before the building was pulled down and before Boots the Chemists moved to the new shopping precinct. The two-way street, now pedestrianized, had many familiar local shops. At number 13, for instance, was the United Cattle Products restaurant and shop. For many years, from the 1930s until the 1960s, there was often a policeman on traffic control duty at the end of the road, as the Market Place was the main thoroughfare through the town.

The other side of Parr's Bank (right) now the Natwest. Directly to the left of this fine building can be seen the Angel Hotel and in the background is Leach's chemists. This 1930s view of the Market Place also shows a policeman on traffic control duty at the end of Chestergate.

The Wheatsheaf Hotel, centre top, was next to the Union Gateway in the Market Place which, in turn, was next to the Town Hall. This bustling market scene was taken in around 1905. Both the Wheatsheaf and the buildings surrounding the oval Union Gateway are now long gone.

A view of the Central Station from Sparrow Park as the building was being demolished to make way for the concrete structure that now stands there. The exact date this photograph was taken was 29 July 1960. Scraggs textile machinery manufacturers building is prominent, centre-right, on Sunderland Street opposite the Queen's Hotel.

An extremely rare photograph of Marlborough College, Tytherington, loaned by Mrs Mason of Bluebell Lane. It is a former private school that was later occupied by the American troops before they left for the D-Day invasion. Marlborough Drive now stands witness to what used to be there.

During February of 1969 the Conservative Association headquarters and Stanley Hall in Castle Street were demolished as part of the town centre redevelopment for the Grosvenor Centre. Here there is a black space where the premises used to be, next door to the County Express buildings which also faced demolition a few days later.

Another part of Tytherington now gone. The old toll bar house at the corner of Bluebell Lane.

Another extremely rare photograph, the only public 'airing' of which has been in Old Macc magazine, of The Cinema, Buxton Road, taken in 1919. Mr Arthur Mellor of Park Lane and his father before him managed the theatre for many years up to its closure in the 1950s. The week's entertainment when this picture was taken featured Tarzan of the Apes and The Romance of Tarzan. These two films, made in 1918, were the very first Tarzan stories screened, and starred Elmo Lincoln in the title role and Enid Markey as Jane.

six

Sports
and
Pastimes

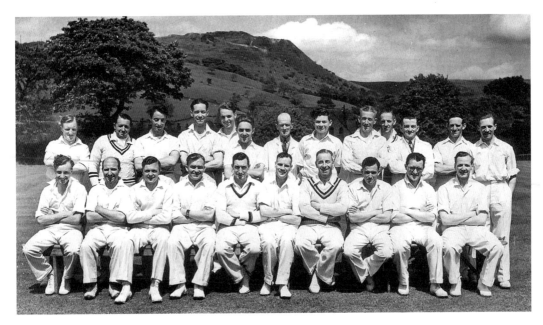

A typical setting on an idyllic day for a local cricket match. With a backdrop of Tegsnose Hill, the venue is Langley Cricket Club's ground after the terrible winter of 1947. This was taken in August of that year and the two teams who took part in the local 'grudge' match were Langley and Macclesfield NALGO (the National Association of Local Government Officers). There was, and still is, a great deal of local cricket played in and around the Macclesfield area and many well-known amateur cricketers are pictured here.

Around the time of the Second World War, Macclesfield Cricket Club first team members stepping out from the pavilion at the Victoria Road ground for a major match in the Cheshire League. The ladies to the front (right) were some of the stalwarts of the club, not only providing their support but glorious sandwiches and cups of tea as well.

St Peter's Gymnastics Club in 1921, proudly displaying the shields and trophies won. The Revd Cholmondley James (with beard) is pictured.

This photograph shows Ernest Twigg winning the British Legion Road Walk in the early 1920s. Mr Twigg is seen crossing the line at Macclesfield Town FC's Moss Rose ground. The old stand is seen to the rear, advertising 'Albert E. Brees, sanitary plumber and electrical engineer'.

This Bullock Brothers photograph of local sportsmen was taken, around 1897, in West Park in front of the famous cannon that came from the Siege of Sebastopol and was melted down during the Second World War. The picture was kindly supplied by Mrs Muriel Massey whose father as a youth (W. Walsh) is among those present. Back row, left to right: T. Edwards, T. Abbott. Centre row: J. Findlow, J. Lawton, J.W. Pratt, A. Fawkner, W. Walsh, C. Pratt, J. Fitchett, J.E. Harrop, T. Bond. Front row: G. Gosling, J. Bradbury, T. Walsh, J.F. Bradbury, W.G. Yates, A.H. Taylor, E. Bloor.

Some Macclesfield Harriers members, shown here in around 1950 at the Talbot Hotel, Chester Road. Back two, left to right: Jim Mottershead and Albert Rigby. Middle three: John Norton, Geoff Hunter, Harry MacLease. Front row: Keith Walton, John Patterson, Jack Higginbotham, John Bowyer, Arthur Evans, Mike Lafferty, Mr Weach (treasurer), Frank Gratton, Stan Cook.

More members of the Harriers, two years later. Included are Arthur Evans, Mike Lafferty, Fred Culley, Dennis Clayton, Derek Sims, Graham Wright, Joe Vare, Geoff Hunter.

Sutton Walking Race was an event that was keenly followed during the years around the Second World War and into the 1950s and 1960s. Here, contestants and other competitors line up outside The Church House at Langley in 1950. The Warren and Barber families are understood to be represented here.

Mr Jack Tempest, a much respected veteran walker, setting off down Jarman from The Church House public house. An idea of how well this walking race was followed is shown by the crowds lining the route, c. 1950.

The West Park, Macclesfield, has for a long time possessed one of the finest crown greens in England, and here an Edwardian Macclesfield family, unfortunately unnamed, takes advantage of the facilities offered.

Gentlemen and lady members of St George's Cycling Club, Macclesfield, taken around 1905 outside St George's schoolrooms.

The Dolphin Inn darts team prior to 1961. Back row, left to right: Joe Reece, George Daniels, Danny Naden, Eddie Brocklehurst, Reg Corbishley. Front row: Jack Goodwin, George Bailey (landlord), Harold Patterson, George Lovenbury. The Baileys retired from the Dolphin pub in 1961.

Another successful Dolphin Inn team, probably not a darts team. Back row, left to right: George Bailey (landlord), Jack Goodwin, Bill Moss, Harry Bailey, –?–, Fred Hill. Front row: Wallace Fare, Les Baguley, –?–, –?–, Albert Stacey, Jack Bailey.

A Macclesfield Central School football team in around 1948. The captain (holding the ball) is Barry Crain and the teacher at the back is Forbes Robinson who went on to be a world-famous opera singer.

North Athletic FC, Macclesfield, the 1946/47 season. Back row, left to right: Mr Coppenhall, Sugden, Lawson, Genders, Bailey, Knight, Bushell. Front row: Batten, Bailey, Walker, Sherratt, Crowder, Coppenhall.

Ernie Foden instructs young Brian Cockayne in the art of 'fisticuffs', c. 1946, at the recently opened Park Green Sporting Club. Eric Gosling is in the background.

Spectators at the Sunday Express Soccer Circle for Boys, attended by the great Stanley Mathews, at the Drill Hall around 1947/8. Third from the right, front row, is Peter Jones, who merely had to cross Bridge Street from his home to attend the function.

A swimming gala at the old Macclesfield Public Baths in Davenport Street, around 1949. These youngsters were obviously the cream of the crop of swimmers from local schools.

Some of the spectators at the swimming gala held at Macclesfield Baths, taken from the shallow end which was three feet six inches deep. Many will no doubt recall the spectators' balcony, with the changing rooms underneath.

One of Macclesfield's most famous bowling clubs was the Pack Horse. This fine green was situated at the rear of the premises of The Jordangate Hotel. Here the gentleman with the pipe is believed to be Edmund Lomas, pictured at the green around 1947. The green and the hotel have now been demolished, and were at the side of what is now the new Macclesfield library.

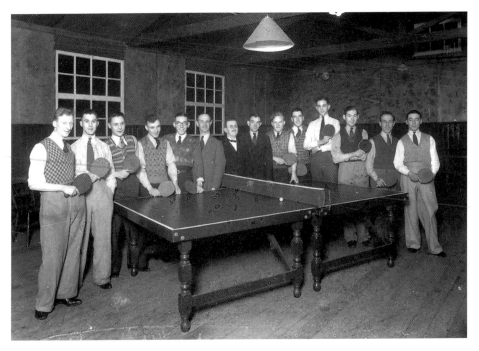

A table tennis tournament photographed by Mr F. Gee. The Brocklehurst Whiston personnel suggests it was taken at the Pavilion, Fence Avenue, Macclesfield, during the 1930s.

Members of Buxton Road Football Club, a long-defunct team, pictured in February of 1913. These young lads could possibly have been a school team or more likely mill apprentices.

St George's FC, the 1917/18 season. Back row, left to right: Revd Winstanley, J. Wilshaw, F. Percival, H. Snape, N. Hall, S. Armitt. Middle row: G. Willitt, T. Longdon, P. Brown, J. Burgess, B. Marton. Front row: H. Holt, A. Cleaver, P. Birchenough, D. Burgess, F. Slater.

Snooker in the snooker room at Macclesfield Conservative Club, Stanley Street, during the late 1940s. The room was the venue for many famous matches and the Conservative Club was a force to be reckoned within local snooker circles for many a year. In fact, now it has moved to its new venue, but there are still many tidy players there.

Above: And now for the distaff side ... some of the 1948 members of Macclesfield Ladies Hockey Club line up before a match.

Hardly a regular Macclesfield pastime, but one which proved to be worthy of note in 1947. Many will no doubt recall the harsh winter we had with the snows starting in late February and blocking off nearly every village and town in the area for weeks. A couple of intrepid Maxonians were photographed using skis as a novel mode of transport down Churchwallgate in Macclesfield. The two gentlemen are not identified but the skier in the foreground looks very much like Edmund Lomas of silk mill fame; however, this is not certain.

Above: A party for employees of Arnolds Mill held at the Stanley Hall, Macclesfield, around the time of the First World War. One of the gentlemen pictured is Mr Jack Winnell, born 1887, who lived as a boy in White Street. He started work at the age of 12 in Langley, walking over The Hollins to commence at 6 am. He attended school at Langley in the afternoon then walked back home to assist the family hand loom weaving business in the evening, carrying out tasks such as winding quills in the family garret. He lived his adult married life in Barton Street and would have been living there at the time this picture was taken.

Left: This remarkable and historic photograph, the property of the Smith family of Lyme Green, shows how families used to work in the garrets of their homes in the town, weaving silk at hand- looms. The picture was taken at 9 Statham Street around 1895-1900 as Thomas Mearn, who came over from Ireland, was working at the loom. At the bottom of the street was the Reform Club.

Here we have one of two photographs taken inside the mill of John Abraham & Brothers Ltd. The finishing department was always a very busy place for these gentlemen.

A hot and steamy place at John Abraham & Brothers Ltd. This was the hank and dye house and it was here that the product the mill was famed for took its colour.

An old and faded photograph of dye hands at Abraham's Mill in 1894. Notice the dye vats in the foreground, one of which is being sat upon by the bowler-hatted gentleman.

Mainly ladies in the making-up department at Abraham's Mill.

Clapham's shirt mill in Athey Street in the early 1900s. Mrs Elsie Winnell (born 1894) is in the centre.
The Winnells were a 'garret family' and had a garret in their White Street home for many years. The
Winnell family walked from Sheffield to Macclesfield in the early 1800s in order to find work. Mrs
Winnell was the wife of Mr Jack Winnell, mentioned with the photograph taken at the Stanley Hall for
employees of Arnolds Mill. Notice the lovely bonnets hanging on the wall and the pinafore dresses worn
by the young ladies.

These gentlemen, as their soot-covered faces testify to, were members of the boiler team at Brocklehurst Whiston's silk mill, Hurdsfield, during the 1930s.

These carts were at the rear of the Queens Hotel in Albert Place around 1910 and were, in fact, being repaired there. But it was not just carts that were repaired there, for thirsts were seen to as well because it was also the site of a brew house.

eight

Events

A procession wends its way up Mill Street, Macclesfield, in 1913, shortly before the 'war to end all wars' began. These starry-eyed gentlemen in the parade are supposedly depicting the mystic Orientals – notice the Geisha Girl who is walking with them. This is thought to be a Rose Queen parade which preceded the carnivals by a good few years. Notice the boy hanging out of the window for a better glimpse and the Silk Warehouse, now demolished, top right. Oh, and not one member of the large crowd of spectators is without a hat!

The young and dashing Air Commodore Arthur Vere Harvey, later Sir Arthur and then Lord
Harvey of Prestbury, at a Macclesfield Conservative Association function. Also shown here are
The Macclesfield Member of Parliament who followed in the footsteps of the Canadian Garfield
Weston, and Mrs Legh of Adlington Hall, the Women's Association Chairman. This could
possibly have been shortly after the 1945 general election.

Air Commodore Harvey arrives at the Conservative HQ, adjacent to the Stanley Hall, where he is
welcomed by delighted supporters who are cheering and clapping him. This is most probably the 1945
election when he was returned as the Macclesfield and Congleton Member of Parliament for the first
time. He retired in the early 1970s and his position was taken by Nicholas Winterton MP.

'Oh, listen to the band'. One of the favourite events on a Sunday afternoon in summer for countless Maxonians was a visit to the park to listen to a brass band playing. Here we see the band in full swing at the West Park bandstand, around 1932.

Another view of the West Park bandstand, but this time in 1903 when Empire Day was being celebrated. The Brocklehurst Museum is in the background.

Opposite below: The Mayor, Cllr M. White, reading the proclamation of the succession to the throne of Princess Elizabeth, in Park Green, Macclesfield.

Above: The crowds turned out in their hundreds, and indeed, thousands, for the visit to Macclesfield in 1949 of the then Princess Elizabeth and her new husband, Prince Philip. The royal couple came by train, alighted at Hibel Road station, and then went on to Brocklehurst Whiston's mill and a reception at the Town Hall. Here we see a sunny Macclesfield crowd awaiting the royal visit in a specially constructed stand outside the Town Hall. The little children at the front have their Union Jacks ready to wave and their red, white and blue paper pom-poms.

'Long Live the Queen' proclaims the banner strung outside the Town Hall. Crowds cheer the band marching past as Macclesfield celebrates the coronation of Elizabeth II in 1953.

Macclesfield's Agricultural Show was an extremely popular event up until the early 1960s and it attracted crowds in their thousands to the South Park. Here we see Alderman J.F. Bex, a Mayor of Macclesfield and Justice of the Peace, talking to a guest at the show, the famous footballer for Stoke City, Blackpool and England, Stanley Mathews, later Sir Stan.

It will be recalled that there were many attractions at the agricultural show, and here we see the Cheshire Division Civil Defence Corps tent, with both Union Jacks and Cheshire Civil Defence flags flying. One well-known member of the Macclesfield Civil Defence was Mr Raymond Maddock.

Macclesfield's troop of the Cheshire Territorial Army, the Terriers, line up around 1950. Danny Norton, bandmaster, with the flat cap is pictured in front and the sergeant behind him is Ernie Foden, a stalwart of the TA and very well known in Macclesfield for his boxing and also through his position in later life as a bailiff.

The banner across Buxton Road says 'Rich is Victoria Park in Beauty' and another one to the right says 'Health to the generous giver'. The occasion was the opening of Victoria Park, a gift to the town by Mr Brocklehurst in the late 1800s.

Meannee Day celebrations were marked by the Macclesfield branch of the Cheshire Regiment Association on 17 February of every year. This was a famous battle in which the Cheshires excelled, and here we see those who took part in the celebrations in 1933 at the Drill Hall, Macclesfield. Major Harris is the dapper little man on the extreme left.

The Mayor of Macclesfield presenting a casket to the Honorary Colonel of the Cheshire Regiment, Lord Newton, when the Cheshire Regiment was given the freedom of the borough at a special ceremony on 2 June 1949. The Town Clerk, Mr Walter Isaac, is the gentleman in the wig and gown. The group is pictured in Waters Green.

Crowds gathered around at the opening of the children's playground in South Park by the Mayor, Cllr Fletcher, in 1935.

The opening of Macclesfield's cenotaph in the newly-landscaped Garden of Remembrance at Park Green in November, 1920. Lt-Col. Bromley Davenport salutes those who have fallen, watched by a large crowd kept within respectful distance.

A wreath is laid at the War Memorial in 1948, watched by the Town Clerk, Mr Walter Isaac, and other civic dignitaries. Park Green brewery can be seen in the background.

Right: Crowds inspect the wreaths laid at the cenotaph in Park Green after the official opening of the memorial in 1920. An ivy-bedecked Park Green chapel is pictured in the background, and those looking at the wreaths clearly depict the fashions of the day.

Below: When the official pharmacy of Macclesfield Co-op, the Macclesfield Equitable Provident Society, opened to the general public in 1948 there was an official opening ceremony, pictured here, attended by the local press and civic dignitaries as well as members of the board of the Co-op.

The collapse of the Bethel Baptist church, at 7 am on Tuesday 6 June 1933. Well-known Maxonian Margaret Lockett provided this picture and her grandfather, the Revd Harry Deal, was the Minister.

What a picture! This is the day when the circus came to town in 1948. These many elephants alighted from special goods wagons at Hibel Road station and walked along Gas Road, across the bottom of Buxton Road and into Waters Green before carrying on to the South Park where the circus was being held. They are pictured passing the cattle pens which were there for many a year. The old Central Station can be seen in the background. The picture was taken from Castle Shoe company's premises. With such an eye-catching parade, there was little need for any publicity for the show . . . and it's a fair bet that rose growers were able to find a good bit of fertilizer as well!

Crowds assemble outside the old Post Office in Park Green, which moved to Castle Street in the 1920s. The occasion for these banner-waving Maxonians is understood to be the thanksgiving service for the end of the First World War and the welcoming home of the Cheshire Regiment.

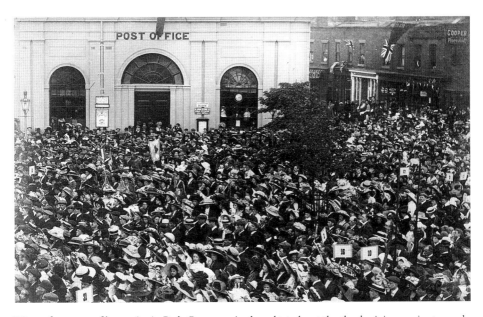

Wave after wave of humanity in Park Green, again thought to be at the thanksgiving service to mark the end of hostilities. Other occasions for a crowd such as this were Empire Day congregations, although in Macclesfield these were held in the Market Place outside the Town Hall.

Cause for celebration in 1937. The event was commonly referred to as the 'Relief of Jordan gate'. After the road surface had been re-laid, cutting Jordangate off for a considerable few weeks, the residents of the area (and there were many in those days) prevailed upon their oldest neighbour, Mr J.T. Wadsworth, to perform their mock opening ceremony. A tape was placed across the road and, outside the George Hotel, he declared the road well and truly open. The moustached gentleman in the doorway is the late Eric Dunkley, a Macclesfield Times reporter of the day, who lived at Hurdsfield. Notice that the hotel served Macclesfield's own Adshead's Ales.

Opposite above: Staff of the General Post Office, Castle Street, Macclesfield, line up for the official photograph taken at their own VE (Victory in Europe) Day celebrations. Most streets and mills in the town had their own celebrations, which were followed later by VJ (Victory in Japan) Day.

Opposite below: As we have already seen, the film So Well Remembered shot on location in Macclesfield by RKO had many Macclesfield extras, and here we see one of the crowd scenes shot at night in the Market Place. The clock, top right, was for many years over Black's gentlemens outfitters shop.

Mr Harry Hayes, local newspaperman and stalwart Methodist, standing (left) by the 'Prefabs', the prefabricated buildings at the bottom of Westminster Road, behind where the shops now stand close to Bollinbrook Road. Mr Hayes, who was strongly connected with Beech Lane Methodist church, is conducting an open-air service and it is presumed that this was a Sunday School service for the children of the estate. The 'Prefabs' lasted until the 1960s, having been built as a temporary measure after the Second World War. They were comfortable homes and many residents were sorry to leave them. Perhaps readers will recall the struggle the families had with the Corporation to provide playing facilities for their children.

Opposite above: Girls of the Central School, Macclesfield, sit down for a celebration meal to mark the Silver Jubilee of George V and his beloved Queen. Little did anyone know that shortly after, in January of 1936, the life of George V would pass swiftly to its close at Sandringham. The popular Prince of Wales became Edward VIII and seemed destined to a kingship of the greatest success until making the vital personal choice: abdication.

Opposite below: A delightful scene showing Macclesfield Prize Silver Band members in around 1948. In the late 1940s the band folded and the musicians transferred their allegiance to the 7th Cheshire Band at the Drill Hall. Holding the baton is Danny Norton, bandsman. Danny was a local cobbler with premises on Cross Street. The man in the trilby hat, centre, is Jack Leonard and the now Margaret Pickford is between the two bandsmen, left.

Players of Macclesfield Town Football Club surrounded by happy supporters after they had received the Cheshire League Challenge Cup, 1948.

Taking a stand. Refurbishment of the Moss Lane stand at Macclesfield FC's Moss Rose ground in 1948.

An event that was not to be missed in 1932. A flying circus came to town and used the Congleton Road airfield, as it was known in those days. The flying circus included clowns who pelted the crowd with flour bombs, acrobats and stunts of all kinds. The airfield was used by light aircraft up until the Second World War and, shortly afterwards, vied with Ringway Farm near Altrincham for the pleasure of providing the North West's new airport. No need to say which won.

The Drill Hall has been the venue for many shows and displays over the years and a very successful one for many years was Macclesfield Model Railway Society's annual displays. This one, in 1961, attracted as many dads as boys.

Brocklehurst Whiston Amalgamated's sports day around 1946/7 at Langley. The lady at the back end of the rope is Alice Hoyle (then Dorothy Allen, now Dorothy Hancock). The next lady is unidentified, then we have Winnie Thompson and finally Marjorie Byrne. No Lycra tracksuits and shorts here ... but plenty of fun. The BWA sports were always eagerly looked forward to, and not only did the mill workers take part but friends and family as well. The post-war era was a good one for Macclesfield silk and its factories, with employment aplenty. Macclesfield was still known as a 'women's town' because of the amount of jobs available in the mills for skilled hands. When man-made fibre came along in strength later, many ladies turned their hands towards this but the advent of ICI and Geigy on the newly-built Hurdsfield Industrial estate put a stop to most of the ancient industry.